# Protecting the public – *your next move*

HSE BOOKS

*© Crown copyright 1997*

*Applications for reproduction should be made in writing to: Copyright Unit, Her Majesty's Stationery Office, St Clements House, 2-16 Colegate, Norwich NR3 1BQ*

*First published 1997*

ISBN 0 7176 1148 5

HS(G)151

*All rights reserved. No part of this publication may be reproduced, stored in a retrieval system, or transmitted in any form or by means (electronic, mechanical, photocopying, recording, or otherwise) without the prior written permission of the copyright owner.*

This guidance is issued by the Health and Safety Executive. Following the guidance is not compulsory and you are free to take other action. But if you do follow the guidance you will normally be doing enough to comply with the law. Health and safety inspectors seek to secure compliance with the law and may refer to this guidance as illustrating good practice.

**ACKNOWLEDGEMENTS**  HSE gratefully acknowledges the help given by the following organisations during consultation on this text:
*Building Employers Confederation*
*EPR Architects Ltd*
*Lovell Construction Ltd*
*Norman & Dawbarn Health and Safety Ltd*
*RGCM Ltd*
*Tarmac PLC*
*Tilbury Douglas Ltd*

# CONTENTS

| | | |
|---|---|---|
| **CONTENTS** | *Foreword* | ...*v* |
| | *Introduction* | ...*1* |
| **SECTION 1** | ***What the law says*** | ...*5* |
| | Health and Safety at Work etc Act 1974 | ...*6* |
| | Construction (Design and Management) Regulations 1994 | ...*6* |
| | Construction (Health, Safety and Welfare) Regulations 1996 | ...*6* |
| | Management of Health and Safety at Work Regulations 1992 | ...*7* |
| | Control of Substances Hazardous to Health Regulations 1994 | ...*7* |
| | Reporting of Injuries, Diseases and Dangerous Occurrences Regulations 1995 (RIDDOR) | ...*7* |
| **SECTION 2** | ***The site perimeter and other boundaries*** | ...*9* |
| | Introduction | ...*10* |
| | Planning provision and maintenance of perimeters | ...*10* |
| | Security precautions | ...*15* |
| | Summary | ...*15* |
| **SECTION 3** | ***Developing authorisation procedures*** | ...*17* |
| | Who you need to authorise | ...*18* |
| | Controlling access to site | ...*18* |
| | Informing visitors | ...*19* |
| | Summary | ...*20* |
| **SECTION 4** | ***Specific hazards, risks and their control - a summary*** | ...*21* |
| | Introduction | ...*22* |
| | Scaffolding and other access equipment | ...*22* |
| | Openings and excavations | ...*24* |
| | Slips, trips and falls within pedestrian areas | ...*25* |
| | Plant machinery and equipment | ...*25* |
| | Hazardous substances | ...*26* |
| | Storing and stacking materials | ...*27* |
| | Electricity and other energy sources | ...*28* |
| | Dust, noise, vibration and sparks | ...*29* |
| | Falling objects | ...*29* |
| | Delivery and other site vehicles | ...*30* |
| | Road works | ...*31* |
| **SECTION 5** | ***Selected groups and premises which need special attention*** | ...*33* |
| | Introduction | ...*34* |
| | The disabled | ...*34* |
| | Children | ...*34* |
| | Occupied premises | ...*37* |
| | Refurbishment of residential properties | ...*37* |
| | Refurbishment of industrial or commercial properties | ...*39* |
| | Health care premises | ...*40* |
| | House building | ...*41* |
| **APPENDIX** | ***Identifying the hazards and evaluating risks*** | ...*43* |
| | Introduction | ...*44* |
| | Risk assessment | ...*44* |
| | Who does what | ...*47* |
| | ***Further reading*** | ...*48* |
| | Additional information | ...*49* |

# FOREWORD

**FOREWORD**

Every year many construction site workers are killed or injured as a result of their work, and others suffer ill health. The hazards are not, however, restricted to those working on sites. Children and other members of the public are also killed or injured because construction activities have not been adequately controlled. The construction industry's performance has improved over the past decade, but the rates of death, serious injury and ill health are still too high.

These deaths, injuries and ill health cause pain and suffering; they also cost money. A recent HSE survey found that 8.5% of the tender price could have been saved, even on a site which had no serious (reportable) injuries.

This booklet is part of HSE's revised series of health and safety guidance for construction. The series will be developed over the next few years. The aim of the series is to help all those involved in construction to identify the main causes of accidents and ill health and to explain how to eliminate the hazards and control the risks. The guidance is simple. It will refer to other relevant documents so that you can build up a clear and comprehensive package.

Each piece of guidance will have general relevance to everyone involved in the construction process, from clients and designers, to contractors and individual workers. But some documents will be particularly relevant to specific groups, depending on the subject they address. All the new guidance will be identified with this logo.

# Protecting the public -
# *your next move*

## INTRODUCTION

**INTRODUCTION**

This guidance is aimed at everyone in construction. It replaces the existing guidance note published by the Health and Safety Executive entitled, *Accidents to children on construction sites*. It provides practical advice on how those designing, planning, managing or carrying out construction work can minimise the risks to the public and others not directly involved. It will be of use to clients, designers, contractors, the self-employed, workers and members of the public.

**1** Each year construction work injures and kills people who have no direct involvement in it. Between 1986 and 1996, construction activities killed 88 members of the public, including 27 children. More than 1250 were seriously injured, of which over 450 were children.

**2** HSE and local authorities receive many complaints from the public concerning construction activities. Some complaints involve actual risks while other complaints pose little risk to health and safety. Some complaints arise directly from nuisance. Such public concern impairs the image of the construction sector.

**3** Most of these accidents and complaints could have been avoided. This publication aims to advise you how. The advice is chiefly concerned with preventing accidents and ill health to the public, but it may also help reduce the incidence of nuisance. This publication identifies the hazards and risks which most commonly affect the public and visitors to sites. It outlines the law that is most relevant to protecting the public and provides advice on how you can comply with your duties. The guidance covers how you can define and maintain the site perimeter and keep the public separated from construction work. It highlights the importance of authorising workers and visitors who come onto your site, even for short periods. It also indicates where problems are most likely to be encountered and suggests ways to control them.

**4** Providing suitable protection for those carrying out construction work will often help protect others who may be affected by it. The precautions which need to be taken to adequately protect the public and visitors may, however, differ from those taken to protect those working on the site. There are good reasons for this. Members of the public may have a lower tolerance than those on site, for example patients in a hospital which is being refurbished may be much less capable of sustaining further impairment to health than healthy people. The public are also less likely to be familiar with the risks associated with construction than those who regularly work in the industry.

**5** Visitors - including experienced construction workers - may also require extra consideration if they are unfamiliar with the layout and particular hazards associated with the site. Certain groups such as children merit special attention because of their particular vulnerability. Certain classes of premises also need special attention because of the nature of the works. This guidance attempts to explain what is reasonable for such special cases by considering particular problems and their solutions.

**6** The guidance does not cover deliberate illegal trespass or forced entry on to sites by protest groups or those intent on criminal activity. However, many of the measures identified here may help. Other enforcement agencies have a role at the public/construction work interface, including the police and local authorities. Their advice may also be helpful.

**HOW TO USE THIS PUBLICATION**

7   The guidance has five sections and an appendix. Section 1 tells you what the law says. The rest provide comprehensive advice on how you can comply with the law. **The advice given in sections two to five is not compulsory.** A number of projects are followed through to illustrate how the advice can be put into practice. The sections can be dipped into according to your needs but reading through all the text will help you gain a more comprehensive picture. Other useful sources of information are highlighted and referenced in the *Further reading* section.

**SECTION 1**   *What the law says*

This section outlines the health and safety legislation which is most relevant to protecting the public from construction work and the authorisation of site personnel.

**SECTION 2**   *The site perimeter and other boundaries*

Excluding people from areas of risk or separating people from construction work. This section explains that most risk assessments will conclude that the site perimeter should be defined by a physical barrier which separates the public from the construction work. Additional barriers may be required in some areas because certain activities present a significant risk outside or inside the site perimeter. The section gives advice on how to construct and maintain suitable barriers.

**SECTION 3**   *Developing authorisation procedures for visitors*

This section provides guidance on systems for protecting those who are allowed access on to site.

**SECTION 4**   *Specific hazards, risks and their control: a summary*

This section looks at the situations which most commonly present hazards and risks to members of the public and gives advice on how they can be controlled. The public will usually be less aware of the hazards than those who work on sites. The extent of the precautions which are necessary to protect the public and contractors in apparently similar circumstances may therefore differ.

**SECTION 5**   *Selected groups and premises which need special attention*

This section identifies the need for particular attention to vulnerable groups such as children, the elderly or disabled. Work in certain premises such as schools or hospitals may also need particular thought and planning. This section provides general advice on dealing with some of these circumstances.

**APPENDIX**   *Risk assessment*

How to use the five steps approach. Two examples are used to illustrate each step.

INTRODUCTION

**SECTION 1**

# What the law says

# SECTION 1 — WHAT THE LAW SAYS

**8** This section identifies the health and safety legislation which is most relevant to protecting the public from construction work. It is not an exhaustive list and you may also have duties under other health and safety legislation. Remember that other legislation also applies to construction work in public areas, for example the New Roads and Street Work Acts 1991, which lays down particular safety requirements for work in the street.

## HEALTH AND SAFETY AT WORK ETC ACT 1974

The Act places a duty on all employers and the self-employed to take reasonably practicable steps to ensure the health and safety of people who are not in their employment, such as members of the public.

The Act also places a duty on employees to co-operate with their employer on health and safety matters and not to do anything which puts others at risk.

## CONSTRUCTION (DESIGN AND MANAGEMENT) REGULATIONS 1994

The CDM Regulations apply to certain types and sizes of construction projects. It requires that health and safety is taken into account and managed throughout all stages of a project, from its conception, design and planning through to site work and subsequent maintenance and repair of the structure.

CDM places a number of duties on those involved in the construction project. Amongst these duties, the client should ensure that the planning supervisor and principal contractor appointed are competent and have made adequate provision for health and safety. This can include such matters as measures to protect the public.

The planning supervisor's duties include ensuring that a pre-tender stage health and safety plan is prepared. This may well include information that relates to the surrounding environment which the principal contractor needs to know about when planning and deciding upon the control measures.

The principal contractor has to ensure that a health and safety plan is prepared for the construction phase, and it is kept up-to-date. There is also a specific duty to ensure that only authorised people are allowed on site and that steps are taken to keep the unauthorised off site. This will require authorisation procedures for visitors and workers and other positive measures to keep others off site.

## CONSTRUCTION (HEALTH, SAFETY AND WELFARE) REGULATIONS 1996

These Regulations impose duties on employers, the self-employed and those in control of construction activities to take reasonably practicable steps to:

- prevent anyone, including members of the public and visitors falling. Where persons are liable to fall more than 2 metres, suitable guard rails and toe-boards or other precautions should be taken;

- prevent materials falling where there is a risk they will strike someone, and also take suitable and sufficient steps to prevent any materials which do fall from striking a person.

Suitable warning signs should be used, where necessary, to prevent danger by identifying the construction site perimeter.

**MANAGEMENT OF HEALTH AND SAFETY AT WORK REGULATIONS 1992**

The Management of Health and Safety at Work Regulations 1992 are intended to improve health and safety management and to detail what is required of employers (and in some cases the self-employed) under the Health and Safety at Work etc Act 1974.

Under the Regulations the employers have to:

(a) assess, in particular, the risks to the health and safety of their employees and of others who may be affected by the work activity. This is for the purpose of identifying the necessary preventative and protective measures. Employers with five or more employees must record the significant findings of this assessment;

(b) co-operate and share information with any other employers who share the same workplace.

**CONTROL OF SUBSTANCES HAZARDOUS TO HEALTH REGULATIONS 1994**

These Regulations place duties on employers who are using substances hazardous to health. There is a wide range of substances which can give a risk to peoples health. Many of these duties extend, not only to employees but to any other person, whether at work or not, who may be affected by the work carried out. Again, this will include members of the public.

**REPORTING OF INJURIES, DISEASES AND DANGEROUS OCCURRENCES REGULATIONS 1995 (RIDDOR)**

These Regulations require that persons having control of premises report certain accidents and dangerous events that occur there. Accidents which result in members of the public being taken to hospital should be notified to HSE (or sometimes the local authority) immediately and followed up by a report on form F2508.

For more detailed guidance on each of the specific legal requirements you are referred to the appropriate publication. Details of this are in the *Further reading* section.

> *You must comply with the law. The remaining five sections in this publication provide advice on how you can do this. However the advice they give is not compulsory and you are free to take any other action which meets your legal obligations.

# SECTION 1     WHAT THE LAW SAYS

SECTION 2

# The site perimeter and other boundaries

# SECTION 2: THE SITE PERIMETER AND OTHER BOUNDARIES

**INTRODUCTION**

**9** This section describes how to plan, provide and maintain suitable perimeters and barriers at locations where it is necessary to separate the public and others from the work. This section also shows how the principles of risk management explained in *Appendix 1* can be implemented after you have identified the hazards which are likely to affect members of the public and visitors. The risk assessment should also indicate where and when risks arise and their significance. The section ends with a simple summary.

**PLANNING PROVISION AND MAINTENANCE OF PERIMETERS**

*Planning*

**10** For most sites the perimeter is a geographical area within which construction work will be carried out. Determining this perimeter is an important aspect of managing public risk. Specific areas of risk may occur within the site such as around deep excavations. Sometimes, construction work can create risks outside the site perimeter, (for example, unloading materials from a delivery lorry outside the perimeter). Three issues need to be considered: **planning** what form the perimeter will take, **providing** the perimeter and **maintaining** what has been provided.

**11** Identifying the issues at pre-tender stage allows specific items to be included in the bill of quantities and it can therefore be included in the pre-tender health and safety plan. This means that prospective principal contractors can take them into account when tendering.

**12** Risk assessment should decide how the perimeters will be defined, what type will be needed to protect the public and where it should be placed. Factors to consider will include:

- the nature and type of the construction work;
- how heavily populated is the area;
- who will need to visit the site during the work;
- whether the site may attract children;
- site characteristics.

*The site perimeter*

**13** On many sites the location of the site perimeter will be obvious. The layout of the site and the site characteristics will influence the position of the site perimeter fencing, for example it may be possible to consider using existing permanent features such as walls, fences or other structures provided they are structurally sound.

**14** It may also be possible to phase the construction of new structures so they will form an effective barrier as the work progresses. Where existing features cannot be used, you will need to decide what materials will form a suitable barrier and where it is required.

*Use of a new structure as part of the perimeter or boundary*

**15** The precautions taken to secure the site perimeter should reflect the level of risk.

**16** The location of site offices will need to be considered in the development of the site and preferably, they should be located near the main site entrance. This allows supervision of those arriving and avoids people having to cross the site, unnecessarily. The entrance and access routes to the site office should be clearly signposted. This is particularly important where there are multiple entrances, where the site is shared, or where the office is located outside the perimeter fencing. Space constraints will affect activities such as site deliveries and off-loading, and may affect the types of construction plant and techniques which can be used.

**17** During the planning of the project certain local issues such as public footpaths or rights of way which may cross the site may be identified. It will be necessary to consider appropriate closure or diversions of these, with the owner, and relevant authorities' consent as early as possible.

> On a project which involved the construction of a new road in a non-urban area, the principal contractor's risk assessment identified that very few members of the public were likely to be in the area and risks from the work were low. Suitable means of demarcating the perimeter of the site using tape and warning signs were erected. However, in certain parts of the site where there was public access, or process risks were higher, additional precautions were taken such as using a 2 metre high fence.
>
> In a shopping precinct, minor construction work involving the painting of timber benches was carried out. The clients, in conjunction with the contractor, decided to provide a barrier although it was not needed on health and safety grounds, but it was felt it was required to prevent people getting paint on their clothes primarily.

# SECTION 2 — THE SITE PERIMETER AND OTHER BOUNDARIES

*Outside the site perimeter*

**18** Construction work can present a risk to the public outside the site perimeter. These risks might include materials falling from access platforms, materials stored temporarily off site, the operation of cranes and other lifting equipment either on or off site. This can change as construction work progresses. The process of risk assessment should have identified these areas as well as any necessary control measures.

*Always ensure that equipment and parts of equipment such as elbows of cranes, excavators, loaders, etc, do not swing into the path of vehicles or pedestrians*

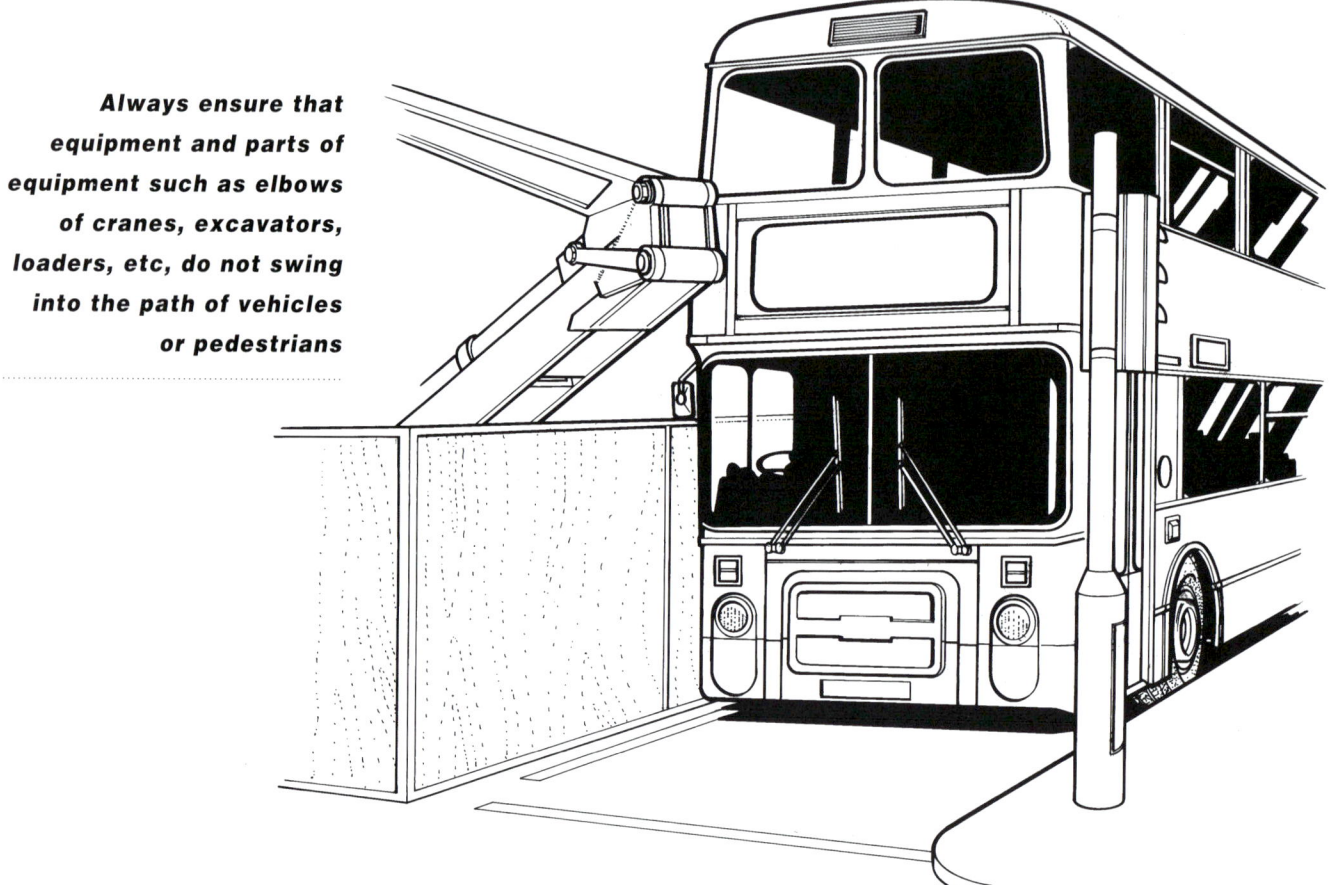

*Within the site perimeter*

**19** Inside the main site perimeter there may be also specific risks which need to be specially controlled, for example around deep excavations or areas where site radiography is taking place. Precautions taken to control the risks might involve excluding contractors and others not directly involved in the work. Areas of risk will change as the work progresses. Risks may also be created at levels above the ground. For example, where mast climbing platforms are used during the external refurbishment of tower blocks, residents opening windows can create a hazard to themselves and the workers at each floor. In these circumstances physical control measures and a safe system of work are necessary to control the risks at higher levels.

### Provision

#### The site perimeter

**20** Experience shows that a 2 metre high fence usually provides a reasonable site barrier, even for short duration work. Perimeter fences can be constructed from a range of materials, including metal mesh. If a fence is to be used then it should be difficult to climb. Using a close mesh which prevents children getting their hands and feet through, should mean that no-one can gain handholds or footholds. Sectional fencing should be locked together and not easily separated without using a tool from the inside of the site. Keep gaps underneath the fence or gate as small as possible to stop anyone gaining access under the fence. Make sure children cannot get access through gaps under temporary fencing. On uneven ground gaps can be quite considerable if steps are not taken to level the surface. Where the feet of sectional fencing points into pedestrian areas, these should be highlighted to avoid tripping hazards.

**21** On plywood, and other similar sheeting materials, wind loading can be considerable and this can be increased by localised environmental conditions. Design the perimeter fencing (including the support and fixing arrangements for the structures) to withstand such conditions. It can be useful to provide public vision panels. These requirements need to be reflected in its design and construction.

**22** Provide securable gates at access points. The gates should form part of the fence and be of the same size. Controlling access through gates is very important. Ensure that the gate can be secured, whether it is open or not, to avoid it being

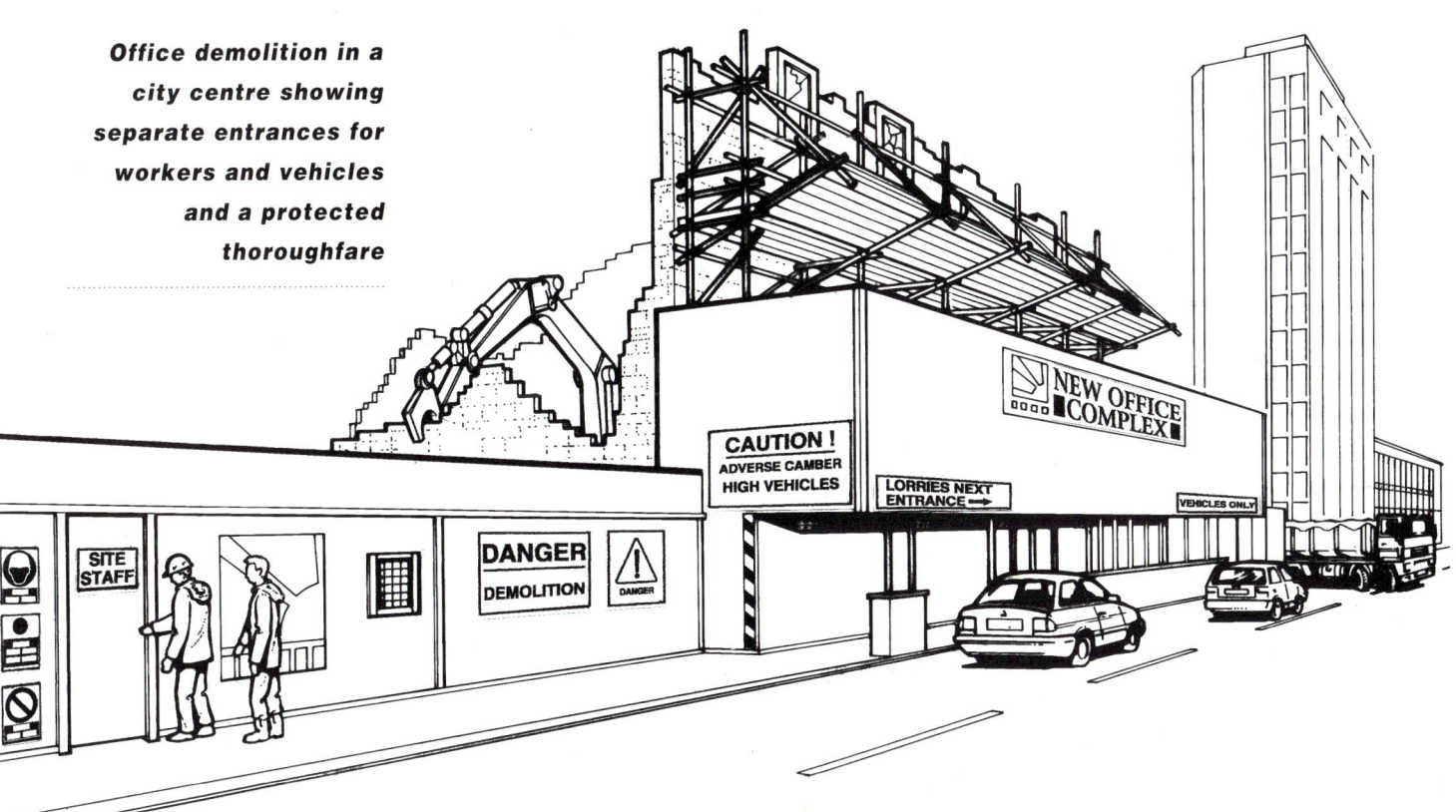

*Office demolition in a city centre showing separate entrances for workers and vehicles and a protected thoroughfare*

# SECTION 2 — THE SITE PERIMETER AND OTHER BOUNDARIES

blown shut in an uncontrolled manner. In some environments, it may also be necessary to close the gates while work is in progress, for example, for reasons of a school's internal security. However, this must not hamper the ability to escape in an emergency. Keep the gate locked and when the site is not occupied secure any temporary fencing.

**23** Site storage compounds should, whenever possible, be big enough to accommodate all the plant, equipment and materials out of working hours. Strict control over the amount and timing of deliveries will help keep storage to a minimum outside the compound area. Sometimes the compound may be in a different area to the main site; it will still need the same levels of protection, signing, etc. Avoid storing materials in a way which allows the fence to be climbed more easily. Some materials pose a significant fire risk and separate, properly constructed, secure compounds may be needed for these materials.

*Outside the site perimeter*

**24** For activities such as the delivery of materials, a banksman may be sufficient to ensure that people outside the site are not put at risk. However, for higher risk activities, for example the use of a crane, it may be necessary to temporarily extend the existing site perimeter while this work is carried out. Alternative pedestrian routes may be required and this will often need permission from the local authority.

**25** It may be necessary to use pedestrian tunnels or properly constructed false ceilings or crash decks to protect the public from falling materials during work over occupied areas.

*Within the site perimeter*

**26** Even if the site has a fence which is designed and constructed so that individuals cannot normally enter, precautions may still be necessary for areas of high risk within the site. This protects those working on the site, visitors and anyone else who may get in. These barriers and precautions should reflect the nature of the risk. For example, where steelwork is being erected, then warning tape, notices and instructions to site personnel to avoid the area may be adequate. However, a strong, physical barrier may be needed to prevent people falling down deep excavations which are likely to be open for a period of time.

## Maintenance

**27** Site perimeters may need to change as the construction work progresses. Plan how you will ensure the perimeters remain current and effective. Control measures may include nominating an individual to manage the perimeter and check it is adequately maintained. If delivery points or the office accommodation is moved, alter the signs accordingly. Review the effectiveness of the control measures. Additional measures will be needed if there is evidence that people can get in. Arrangements for maintaining the perimeter should be included in the construction phase health and safety plan where CDM applies.

## SECURITY PRECAUTIONS

**28** Many of the precautions taken to prevent access will improve site security. However, the use and location of extra 'security-only' measures such as barbed wire or razor wire, needs careful consideration. Accidental contact needs to be prevented. Therefore, the use of security wire should usually be restricted to around internal compound fences at a height in excess of 2 metres. Where it is used around the perimeter, provide warning signs to make sure people know it is there. Other security precautions, including surveillance equipment such as closed circuit TV and infra-red systems, are useful deterrents.

**29** If security guards are employed on either a permanent or visiting basis, they will often work alone. You should provide information about site risks to their employer and co-operate with them. If they patrol the site, the principal contractor should ensure there is safe access, plus a well-illuminated route, and clear information including any changes to the site.

**30** Security staff may need to move around the site, so select and position the lighting to ensure that signs are readable and that shadows do not mask hazardous areas. Lighting is a good means of deterring those who wish to gain unauthorised access to the site.

**31** For advice on site security and how to prevent trespass, contact the local police crime prevention officer.

### Summary

1  Plan by:
- identifying the hazards;
- assessing the risk;
- eliminating risk from construction operations by design or other means if reasonably practicable;
- defining the area to be protected;
- identifying what is required at the site perimeter and other areas where people may be at risk, for example:
  - 2 metre sectional fencing closed mesh;
  - 1 metre fence;
  - 2 metre fencing broad mesh;
  - security cameras;
  - security guards.

2  Provide by:
- erecting the protection making use of any existing site features, for example buildings, walls, etc;
- erecting warning/information signs.

3  Maintain by:
- implementing procedures for regular inspection, maintenance, etc;
- reviewing in the light of experience and modify accordingly.

# SECTION 2
## THE SITE PERIMETER AND OTHER BOUNDARIES

SECTION 3

# Developing authorisation procedures

# SECTION 3  DEVELOPING AUTHORISATION PROCEDURES

**32** Many people will visit the site during construction work. Under CDM, the principal contractor needs to take reasonable steps to ensure that only authorised persons are allowed on to site. However, some clients may have specific rules which will need also to be incorporated within the authorisation procedures, for example where construction work is taking place within the client's premises. But even where CDM does not apply, persons in control of a construction site need to have a system for ensuring the health and safety of all those who visit. The sophistication of these precautions should reflect the size, risks and complexity of the site and the work; what is suitable for a major project may be quite inappropriate for a small one. While other sections of this publication focus on public protection, this section is chiefly concerned with managing and controlling access for workers and visitors. This section provides examples of authorisation procedures and explains how these can be operated.

## WHO YOU NEED TO AUTHORISE

Workers:

- those carrying out work on the construction site.

Visitors who will normally fit into one of the following categories:

- people who have some involvement in the construction process, for example client representatives, members of the design team, delivery drivers and utility companies;

- those whose work on site is part of a regulatory process and have a statutory right of entry such as building control officers, HSE or local authority inspectors;

- those who work on the site, but are not directly engaged in construction work, such as sales staff, security staff, etc;

- possible future occupiers;

- the general public (including those who may come on site in search of work).

## CONTROLLING ACCESS TO SITE

**33** Controlling access begins at the site entrance. The entrance(s) should be clearly marked and separate access routes provided for pedestrians and vehicles. Ensure that visitors and workers report their presence as soon as they arrive. Use signs or other means to direct them to a fixed control or reporting-in point. Make sure they have a safe means of getting there. On a small site, the site hut will probably act as the control point but on a large site with more frequent visitors it might prove useful to set up a special security booth. Do not allow visitors and workers to walk around unaccompanied unless they are familiar both with the site and the risks they may be exposed to.

**34** Keep a record of who is on site and when they arrive and depart. This helps track people in an emergency and can reduce risk to the emergency services. It can also improve the security of plant and materials. On a large and complex project a 'pass' scheme or swipe card could be established so that only those who have a pass are allowed on to the site. A precondition requirement for authorisation (or obtaining a pass) could be enforced, for example everyone could be given site awareness training before they start work on site. On smaller projects it may only be necessary for people to report to the site agent or supervisor to gain that authorisation. On small sites, a simple log book usually suffices. Recording who is on site is an important means of communicating vital health and safety information.

**35** Issuing some means of identification at the control point allows you to check quickly and easily whether someone is authorised to be on site or in a particular area. Some contractors have provided visitors with a badge or a distinctive coloured hard hat, highlighting their presence.

## INFORMING VISITORS

### Provision of information

**36** At the control point those new to the site can be given relevant information and any necessary training about special rules, specific hazard areas, emergency procedures, etc. This can include any changes which may have occurred since they last arrived. These procedures could be covered in any site rules in the health and safety plan.

> **A steel erection contractor prepared a safety method statement which included information about the health and safety risks to those not involved in the work. The principal contractor incorporated this information into the induction training given to all visitors and other contractors whilst the work was being carried out.**

**37** Information alerts visitors to the potential risks, site rules, etc. However, where visitors are unfamiliar with the site layout, or sites are very large or the work presents significant risks, it may be necessary to accompany them at all times on site.

**38** Risk assessment should identify all necessary personal protective equipment (PPE), such as safety helmets and boots, which any visitor should wear. Everyone allowed on to the site must wear the appropriate PPE. The site should carry surplus equipment for known or likely visitors. If the visit is by prior arrangement, advise visitors what is expected of them.

> **A new housing project had a completed show home at the front of the development. It was separated from the rest of the site and had unrestricted access. The company's policy stated that prospective customers had to be accompanied by a member of the sales staff if they wished to view the actual location of their own house. Appropriate PPE was provided and had to be worn. Sales staff had to obtain permission from the site manager before entering the site where the work was being carried out. The Company had a policy of encouraging visitors to come when work was not in progress, such as at weekends.**

# SECTION 3: DEVELOPING AUTHORISATION PROCEDURES

> A group of medical staff wanted to visit the site during the construction of a new medical department. The principal contractor wrote to the client before the visit advising of the necessary protective equipment. The visitors chose to provide their own protective clothing and footwear but did not bring hard hats. The principal contractor provided hard hats and gave the visitors the necessary induction training before the accompanied tour began.

**39** Some work of a particularly hazardous nature may need to carried out under a formal permit-to-work (PTW) system. Such work is not within the scope of this guidance.

> An industrial radiography company carried out non-destructive testing of welds on a site. A permanent record of the tests was required. The work involved the use of ionising radiation. Although the work was done out of hours the area was taped off, and warning notices and lights were erected. The company patrolled the taped perimeter to ensure only those actually carrying out the work entered the area.

**40** Make sure your authorisation procedures are implemented and that they remain effective as the work progresses.

---

### Summary

1 Implement an authorisation system for visitors, and ensure those who operate it understand it. This should include:
- a readily identifiable reporting-in point;
- providing safe access between the site entrance(s) and the control point;
- making sure the route between the entrance and the reporting-in point is clearly marked;
- providing appropriate information on the site rules, hazards and special precautions,
- PPE;
- ensuring people are accompanied around site, and issued with ID if needed.

2 Ensure the scheme matches the precautions to the risks, and is adapted as these risks alter.

3 Monitor and review the scheme, as necessary.

### SECTION 4

# Specific hazards, risks and their control - a summary

# SECTION 4: SPECIFIC HAZARDS, RISKS AND THEIR CONTROL - A SUMMARY

## INTRODUCTION

**41** Many of the hazards discussed in this section will be familiar to those who plan and manage health and safety on site. Risk assessments will identify whether precautions over and above those taken to protect site workers should be taken to protect others. The section outlines common hazards and the precautions needed to control the risks to members of the public and visitors. It is not an exhaustive list; your work may present other hazards which need to be controlled.

## SCAFFOLDING AND OTHER ACCESS EQUIPMENT

### Problems

**42** The erection, dismantling and use of scaffolding and other access equipment, for example mobile elevating work platforms, present various risks because persons outside the site can be struck by:

- components which are being moved across a public area during erection or dismantling;
- components which fall during erection or dismantling;
- stored materials or debris which fall off or through gaps in the working platform (this can be a particular problem where the building facade is curved or is not flat);
- scaffolding and other equipment which collapses because it is not properly designed, erected or secured;
- plant or equipment which collapses as a result of instability or following impact;
- moving parts of mobile access equipment erected in an area to which the public have access.

Where access equipment is not adequately fenced off people may also:

- walk into or otherwise make contact with access equipment;
- gain access on to the equipment and then fall off or through the working platform or ladder;
- use the equipment to gain access to other elevated areas and subsequently fall from there;
- use debris chutes as slides.

These last three issues are often a particular problem with children.

### Precautions

**43** You will need to liaise with the local highways authority, and may need authorisation from them if your work involves the closure or obstruction of public footpaths or roads. You will probably need a licence from them before you can begin. The licence may set standards which describe aspects of how a scaffold should be constructed, how it should be marked (paint, tape, etc), and when it needs to be lit. But regardless of this, there are always certain precautions which you can take:

- exclude the public from the work area whenever possible;

- fence off the area and provide alternative routes which are clearly signposted and avoid additional crossing of the road wherever possible;

- erect, modify and dismantle equipment when there will be fewer members of the public in the area and always use warning notices;

- fans, tunnels and sheeting are a useful means of protection. Make sure the scaffold is designed to take the extra loading and wind resistance;

- ask for protective measures to be put in place at an early stage during erection and have them removed as late as possible during dismantling;

- lighting may be necessary in tunnels;

- use brick guards, netting or other suitable protection to prevent materials falling;

- do not drop or throw components during erection or dismantling;

- make sure the working platform is constructed to prevent materials falling through it, for example double board scaffold platforms and insert a layer of strong polythene between the two sets of boards (a few small punctures will permit rainwater to drain away);

- make sure scaffold components do not project where there is a risk to people or vehicles;

- bolts on couplings should face away from the public or be wrapped;

- consider enclosing the base of the scaffolding to prevent climbing, especially on or near occupied residential premises and schools. Consider the use of anti-climbing paint;

- out of hours, remove ladders from the scaffold. Secure them in a compound or in storage containers;

- ensure that doors to buildings or those allowing access to roof or lift motor rooms, etc, are locked at all times when work is not in progress, for example during lunch breaks, at the end of shifts and at weekends;

- consider using alternatives to scaffolding such as mobile elevating work platforms, cradles and mast climbers. These can reduce the likelihood of people gaining access to heights providing the equipment is properly isolated when not in use;

- debris chutes should be protected either by providing lids or covers, etc.

> **A local authority wanted double glazed windows installed in its high-rise flats. The pre-contract document stated that the contractor would need to use mast climbing work platforms or similar, rather than traditional scaffold to reduce the likelihood that residents or others would climb on to the working platform from balconies. The successful contractor was also contractually obliged to take steps to prevent the equipment being tampered with.**

# SECTION 4 — SPECIFIC HAZARDS, RISKS AND THEIR CONTROL - A SUMMARY

**OPENINGS AND EXCAVATIONS**

## Problems

**44** Persons can be injured if they fall:

- into excavations, manholes or other holes in the ground;
- over open edges such as stairwells or open floor edges;
- on to pointed metal or timber objects such as projecting reinforcement bars.

They may also drown if they fall into deep excavations where water has gathered or otherwise be injured because they cannot see around or through physical precautions taken to reduce other risks.

## Precautions

**45** The risk of injury can be reduced in a number of ways:

- shore or batter excavations to prevent accidental collapse of the sides;
- provide guard rails and toe-boards or similar where it is possible to fall 2 metres or more;
- barriers such as chestnut paling or similar may prove adequate where the excavation is shallower;
- barriers should preferably be placed at least a metre away from the edge of the excavation;
- securely fixed marked covers may also be used;
- protect openings, shafts, etc, from approaching traffic;
- plan and control the work so that you are able to back-fill as soon as possible and where possible, do not leave the excavation open overnight;
- do not pile materials or spoil on to pavements forcing pedestrians into the road. Clean up as soon as possible;
- make sure that any precautions do not obscure the view of pedestrians and drivers. Use vision panels in solid barriers or keep their heights to a level that people can see over.

**SLIPS, TRIPS AND FALLS WITHIN PEDESTRIAN AREAS**

### Problems

**46** Slips, trips and falls are a frequent source of injury to members of the public. Inadequate protection of holes, uneven surfaces, poor re-instatement, trailing leads and cables, spillage of oils, gravel, etc, are just some of the causes. Poor storage of materials and equipment, and other obstructions in public areas, including inadequate control of waste materials in public areas are other common causes.

### Precautions

**47** The risks can be reduced in the following ways:

- segregate or control access to the work area by physical barriers or warning signs. If tape is used ensure this does not become a tripping hazard itself;

- work during hours when the public is less likely to be in the area;

- provide clear signs and proper protection at obstructions;

- use temporary flooring material, for example plywood or steel plates, to cover uneven ground or potholes;

- avoid trailing cables (especially on stairways). Cover or fix any which need to cross pedestrian areas;

- provide lighting at night and in dark areas;

- remove waste and rubbish as it arises;

- reinstate surfaces properly and as soon as work is complete;

- clear all spillages and obstructions from public routes as soon as possible and always before the public are allowed access to the area again.

> A shopping centre was being refurbished. Repair work to the floor was done outside shopping hours. During the day, the whole area was covered by a substantial plywood sheet and rubberised matting to provide a safe, level walking surface.

**PLANT MACHINERY AND EQUIPMENT**

### Problems

**48** The authorised and unauthorised use of plant and equipment presents a range of hazards. Almost any piece of plant is dangerous in the wrong hands and some plant can be started easily without the proper keys or tools.

### Precautions

**49** The risks can be reduced in the following ways:

- all plant should be immobilised out of hours;

- remove keys and starting handles and try to store them in a compound or similar secure area;

# SECTION 4 — SPECIFIC HAZARDS, RISKS AND THEIR CONTROL - A SUMMARY

- cab covers also make vehicles more difficult to enter;

- place excavator buckets, lift truck forks, etc, on the ground at the end of the day;

- do not drive forklift trucks along public roads with the forks raised too much. The driver should have a clear view;

- avoid lifting across public areas if possible;

- properly support and chock bowsers to prevent accidental displacement;

- check that all plant and equipment operatives are competent;

- remove cartridge guns and cartridges from site where possible, or lock them up at the end of the day. Clear up all used and misfired cartridges at least daily - accidents have occurred when children have struck unfired cartridges which have been left on site.

## HAZARDOUS SUBSTANCES

### Problems

**50** Members of the public and visitors may be affected by the poor storage, transportation, use or disposal of hazardous substances. Other substances cause ill health effects when they are inhaled, swallowed or when they come into contact with the skin or eyes. Flammable liquids and gases can cause fires or even explosions. Some substances and materials, such as foams, give off toxic fumes when burned.

### Precautions

**51** The precautions taken to protect workers from these substances will often reduce the risk to everyone else:

- use less hazardous materials if possible, for example water rather than solvent based paints;

- change the way work is done, for example use water suppression or local exhaust ventilation where dusts are created;

- apply solvent based paints or adhesives by brush rather than spraying;

- exclude everyone not directly involved in the work from the vicinity, this can be particularly necessary during wood worm and damp proof chemical treatments;

- plan and control the amounts ordered and delivered;

- limit the amount of flammable or hazardous substances handled or used on site at any one time;

- only decant hazardous materials into suitable, properly marked containers;

- collect and dispose of notionally empty containers;

- store all hazardous substances in suitable containers or in secure compounds when not in use.

**STORING AND STACKING MATERIALS**

### Problems

**52** The storage of materials presents several hazards:

- materials may fall from storage areas, scaffolds or other working platforms;
- pallets and manhole rings may topple or otherwise move;
- part-opened pallets and badly stored bricks can topple;
- certain materials which are stored horizontally and not secured can move in high winds, for example open packs of roofing sheets stored on roofs;
- materials which are stored upright can topple over, for example unsupported roof trusses propped against a wall;
- piles of sand, gravel, earth, etc, may shift burying those who are climbing on them or nearby;
- people can fall from the top of storage areas, stacks, etc. They may also be used as a means of climbing on to other positions of danger;
- the public may be struck by materials and plant or exposed to hazardous substances;
- during the transfer of materials between off-site storage areas and the site.

### Precautions

**53** The risks associated with the storage of materials can be reduced in several ways:

- store materials within the site perimeter, preferably in secure compounds or away from the perimeter fencing. The area should be well lit to discourage unauthorised entry;
- pallets should be stored on level ground, no more than three high. Remember the contents of pallets become less stable once the packaging is broken;
- prevent manhole rings and similar materials rolling. Store them on their end rather than chocking them. Store them on level ground, no more than two high;
- store materials such as roofing sheets and plywood horizontally, make sure they are firmly secured to prevent them being blown away, especially when they are stored at height;
- vertical stacks of materials and materials stacked against walls, etc, need to be propped or secured to prevent them toppling. Purpose built storage frames may be appropriate;
- make sure loose materials stored on platforms or other similar areas cannot fall accidentally. Toe-boards and brick guards should be in place. Materials should not be stacked above the height of the brick guards;
- limit the height of all material stacks;
- avoid leaving vertical faces on sand piles;

# SECTION 4 — SPECIFIC HAZARDS, RISKS AND THEIR CONTROL - A SUMMARY

- prevent items such as scaffolding tubes from falling or toppling over. If it is impracticable to store them other than vertically, even for a short period, then take steps to ensure they do not topple over;

- avoid storing materials off-site where possible. If it is unavoidable, position storage areas away from busy public routes, and keep distances between stores and the site as short as possible. Post warning signs.

**ELECTRICITY AND OTHER ENERGY SOURCES**

## Problems

**54** Energy sources on site present a range of hazards:

- contact with electrical supplies or arcing can cause shock, burns and even death;

- bottled gas can cause fires or explosions if they are not stored safely or if they are tampered with;

- fuel and gas oil can also ignite causing burns.

## Precautions

**55** These risks can be reduced at the planning stages and while work is being carried out in the following way:

- use a suitably protected supply, cordless tools or reduced voltage equipment, for example 110 V centre tapped. For other purposes such as lighting, it may be possible to use even lower voltages;

- place lights out of reach and other parts of the electrical system which may expose people to danger;

- make sure gas cylinders and appliances are fitted with valves which require special tools to turn on the supply;

- isolate gas cylinders when not in use and lock them in a secure cage out of hours;

- secure cylinders to prevent them toppling;

- secure bowsers in a stable frame and padlock them off;

- avoid lighting fires. Remember some substances give off toxic fumes when burned. Make sure that any fires which are lit are properly extinguished well before the end of the day.

> **A delivery driver arrived at site with his two children in the cab. As he began raising his tipper, it came into contact with an 11 kV overhead line. The controls in the lorry cab began to burn and in a panic to rescue his children, the driver climbed up to the cab. He was electrocuted as he touched the cab handle. The children escaped by jumping away from the lorry.**

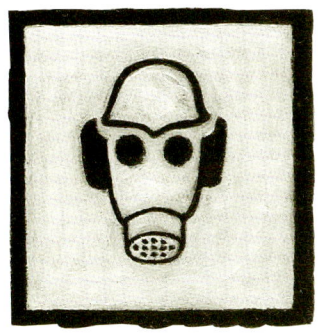

**DUST, NOISE, VIBRATION AND SPARKS**

### Problems

**56** Noise, dust and vibration do not usually pose a health risk to members of the public if their exposure is likely to be low and of a short duration. They can, however, cause serious inconvenience especially in urban areas. Sparks may cause minor burns if they make direct contact with the skin or clothes. Noise, dust and vibration are a frequent source of complaint.

### Precautions

**57** The controls adopted to protect the workforce will often reduce the risk of the nuisance to others:

- use noise suppression on equipment;
- adopt different work methods, for example when cutting paving slabs, consider the use of guillotines rather than disc cutters;
- use stacks of materials or existing features as temporary noise barriers;
- use low dust products;
- use water suppression or exhaust ventilation;
- carry out the work off site;
- work at times when the public are less likely to be in the area;
- provide solid barriers adjacent to public areas.

> A company was carrying out street works involving the use of road cutting saws and disc cutters. Hardboard sheets were fixed to the fence on the site perimeter to prevent sparks and stone chips going into pedestrian areas.

### Problems

**58** Members of the public have been seriously injured and even killed after being struck by falling or ejected materials.

### Precautions

**59** Priority must be given to stopping materials falling in the first place. When you have done what you can to achieve this, you then need to take steps to stop people being struck by any materials which do fall as follows:

- always plan how materials will be raised and lowered;
- do not throw materials into an uncontrolled area and use chutes for debris;
- provide an enclosed hoist platform and carefully position gin wheels, etc. If possible, avoid working above a public area;

**FALLING OBJECTS**

# SECTION 4 — SPECIFIC HAZARDS, RISKS AND THEIR CONTROL - A SUMMARY

- ensure there are safe systems of work when dismantling equipment, for example striking formwork or dismantling scaffolds to prevent components and timbers falling into public areas;

- provide debris netting to trap small pieces of ejected material;

- keep material storage to a minimum; provide brick guards and never store materials above the height of the brick guards;

- protected walkways may be needed in some circumstances, for example demolition sites where materials could fall into pedestrian areas;

- where it is not possible to eliminate the risk of materials falling or being ejected, the area should be fenced off or at least demarcated. Only authorised people should enter and even their access should be controlled to avoid times when there is a risk of them being struck;

- identify areas of risk and put up warning signs.

**DELIVERY AND OTHER SITE VEHICLES**

## Problems

**60** Delivery and other moving site vehicles create several hazards:

- pedestrians may be struck by vehicles entering or leaving the site;

- site and delivery vehicles may obstruct the pavement forcing pedestrians into the road where they can be struck by other vehicles;

- vehicles may strike non-site vehicles whilst entering or leaving the site;

- unsecured loads may fall off, striking pedestrians or other vehicles;

- unauthorised use of vehicles which are not switched off or locked when the driver is not in the cab;

- vehicles may take contaminated material off site on their wheels;

- delivery vehicles may also enter site with children in the cab.

## Precautions

**61** It is important to consider access and approaches to the site during the planning stage; think about the proximity of schools, hospitals, etc, and possible busy periods. The risk to pedestrians and drivers of other vehicles can be reduced in several ways:

- segregate pedestrians and vehicles wherever possible;

- avoid crossing traffic flow. Divert site traffic away from pedestrianised areas and built-up housing estates, if possible;

- minimise reversing on to roads or public areas;

- control stocks to make sure you have the right materials at the right time;

- wherever possible, provide adequate space on site for off-loading vehicles;

- if you have to load or unload vehicles across the pavement, make sure there is safe access for pedestrians and other vehicles;
- allow sufficient clearance around mobile loading arms;
- choose delivery times which avoid busy pedestrian or traffic periods;
- use a banksman to direct vehicles and to assist with loading and unloading;
- give delivery companies advance notice of routes to follow or avoid, and loading/unloading arrangements, etc;
- discourage drivers bringing children on to site. If this is unavoidable, prohibit children leaving the cab, at all times, unless they can go to a safer place;
- ensure loads are properly secured;
- provide wheels washes and make sure drivers use them before leaving contaminated sites;
- secure vehicles and plant when not in use. If possible, leave them in a secure area overnight and immobilise them.

**ROAD WORKS**

### Problems

**62** Both the New Roads and Street Works Act 1991 and chapter 8, *Traffic signs manual*, sets out the requirements for signing and lighting for work in the highways. Whilst this may help reduce the risk to members of the public, they address only a small range of the hazards created by road and street works. Many of these have already been dealt with on an individual basis in other parts of this section but it is worthwhile emphasising them again because the work is usually carried out very close to the public. The hazards are as follows:

- members of the public can be struck by slewing arms or counter-balances on plant reversing vehicles and by falling paving slabs, flying road chips or other materials;
- poor storage of materials and poor re-instatement can cause slips and trips. It can also force pedestrians into the road where they are at risk of being struck by traffic;
- pedestrians can fall down inadequately fenced excavations;
- some of the chemicals used in road building and repair can cause risks to health.

### Precautions

**63** Road and street works tend to be very mobile and the site perimeter can change very rapidly. Procedures for maintaining the perimeter and other control measures need to address this. The precautions are as follows:

- select plant which is suitable for the work and the site. Mini-excavators, etc, may need to be used in small sites to prevent the public being struck during slewing operations;

# SECTION 4 — SPECIFIC HAZARDS, RISKS AND THEIR CONTROL - A SUMMARY

- use trained banksmen to supervise the movement of vehicles;

- draw the public's attention to the work by using the correct signs, lights and information boards. Consider making works vehicles and plant more conspicuous by highlighting jibs, etc;

- re-instate excavations as quickly as possible. Fence off those which need to remain open;

- prevent tripping by covering uneven surfaces or alerting the public to their presence;

- do not stack large quantities of paving slabs upright. Avoid storing them near entrances and busy pedestrian areas;

- store materials within the site perimeter, preferably in a separate compound away from any perimeter fencing;

- remove plant and equipment from site at the end of the shift. If this is not possible, isolate and secure it;

- select and use the least hazardous materials and chemicals. Use tools fitted with dust and noise suppression. Use enclosures around dusty and noisy equipment.

> **Where membrane sprays containing isocyanate are being used, there is little risk to drivers provided they keep moving; however, once the traffic stops the risk is higher. Therefore spraying may need to stop if the traffic does; this needs to be made clear in the site procedures.**

**SECTION 5**

# Selected groups and premises which need special attention

# SECTION 5 — SELECTED GROUPS AND PREMISES WHICH NEED SPECIAL ATTENTION

**INTRODUCTION**

64 Some groups, such as the disabled, elderly and children, require special attention. Work in certain premises, including schools and hospitals, also requires careful thought and planning. This section provides more detailed advice on some of these specific areas. Some of the detailed suggestions in individual parts of this section will be relevant to other environments.

**THE DISABLED**

65 The disabled are especially at risk where construction work affects pedestrian routes, for example TV cable installation or scaffold erection on pavements. It is therefore important to identify whether your work will affect a route which is regularly used by people with disabilities. Do wheelchair users pass frequently? Could blind people be at risk? The Highways Act 1980 and the New Roads and Street Works Act 1991 apply in pedestrian areas and roads. They set out certain procedures which need to be followed and precautions which need to be taken, for example lighting of scaffolds and waste skips, reinstatement of footpaths, etc. This legislation emphasises the need to take account of vulnerable groups. It is important to seek advice from the local authorities.

**CHILDREN**

66 The death or injury of a child is a particularly tragic event, so a lot of effort needs to be given to keeping them out of the site and away from any areas of danger. Children have vivid imaginations. They often see construction sites as playgrounds where they can act out favourite games, films, TV programmes or cartoons.

> **A tree on a new housing estate under construction had a rope hanging from it. Local children had used this as a swing for much of the summer. As work progressed, no-one on site thought anything more about it. One afternoon a child swinging on the rope fell to the ground, and was pierced on metal starter bars sticking up from the newly laid foundations.**

67 Site occupiers may find it useful to liaise with local schools, tenants associations, etc. HSE has produced a video called *Game Over*, dealing with the risks of children on site. Let them know what the work programme is and what risks are associated with construction work. Discuss how children can be made aware of the dangers and kept off site: ask for their advice. Sending letters to nearby households can be a useful way of informing residents about work. Talking to children and showing films or videos will raise awareness and can help reduce accidents, trespass and vandalism. However, these events can backfire and may actually encourage children to try and get on to site rather than deter them. Their content needs to be very carefully thought out to avoid this. The local police force may agree to participate in similar activities.

68 Site management should make subcontractors, delivery drivers and other visitors aware of all restrictions regarding children before they arrive on site. This is particularly important during the school holidays when children may be more likely

to ride in delivery lorries with their parents. Suitable steps should be taken to ensure that everyone observes the site rules about children.

**69** Work on school premises often requires the highest standards of public protection: for example, 2 metre plywood panels may need to be fixed around the base of scaffolds to prevent children climbing onto them. Tunnels and fans may be necessary near playgrounds and entrances to prevent pupils, staff and parents being struck by falling objects.

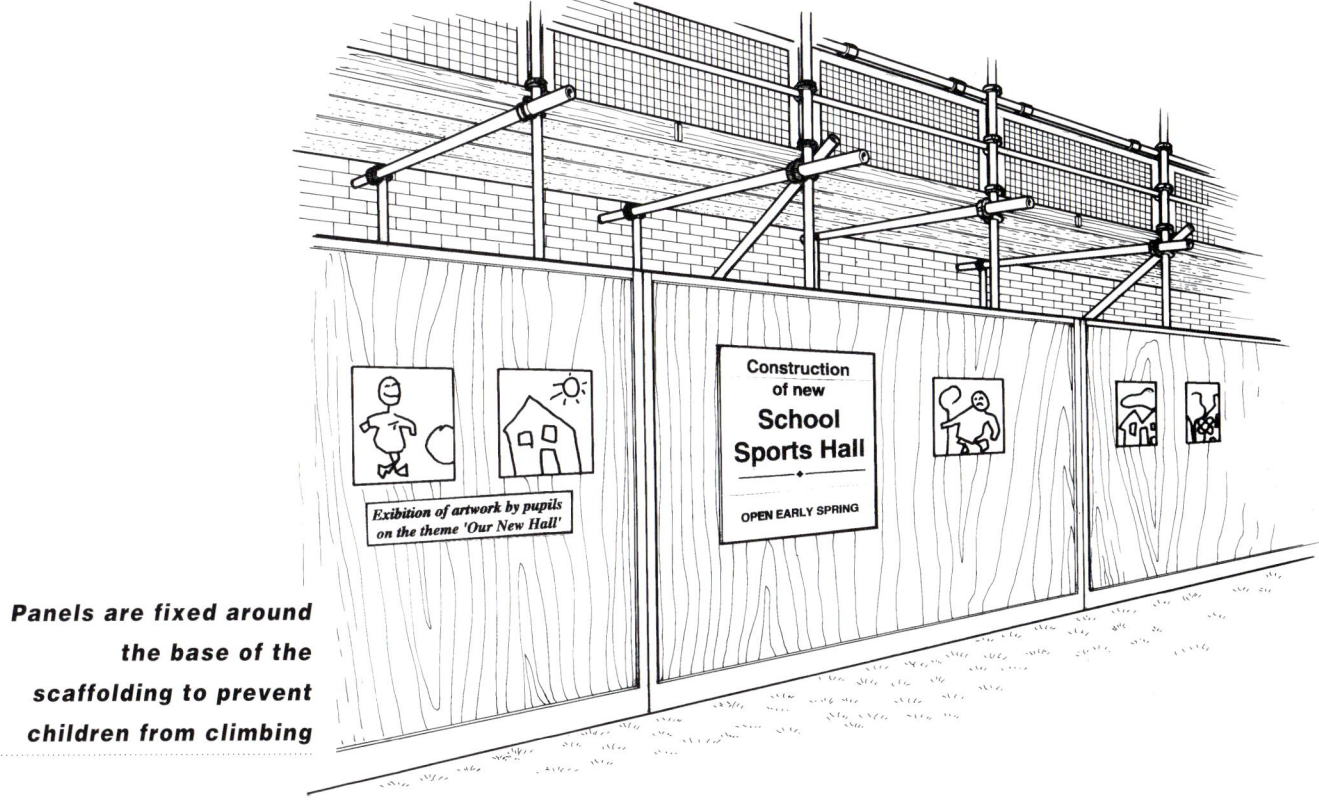

**Panels are fixed around the base of the scaffolding to prevent children from climbing**

**70** Local authorities and school governing bodies will usually have procedures for controlling construction activities. Contractors should familiarise themselves with these and develop systems to meet their requirements during the earliest stages of project planning.

**71** Whenever possible, projects or activities which present high risks to staff and pupils should be carried out during school holidays, at weekends or out of school hours. If this is not possible, the work should be programmed to avoid busy periods such as school start, finish and break times. Deliveries should also be arranged to avoid these times.

**72** It is important to liaise closely with the school throughout the work. Informal talks and video presentations by site personnel will help alert staff and pupils to the dangers and help them understand why the precautions are necessary.

**73** Some contractors have also organised site visits as a means of educating pupils and staff. Again these events need to be carefully planned to avoid encouraging

# SECTION 5 — SELECTED GROUPS AND PREMISES WHICH NEED SPECIAL ATTENTION

children on to site. School staff, governors and parents should be consulted and their agreement obtained before any visits take place. Children and staff should have all necessary protective equipment and not be exposed to any significant health and safety risks while on site. This will often mean that certain work activities cannot be carried out during the visit. Both staff and pupils should be tightly supervised throughout the visit.

**74** The Health and Safety (Young Persons) Regulations 1997 specifically address the issue of work experience. Guidance to these regulations can be found in *Young people at work*.

> On a large project, the construction of a new art gallery and museum, an elevated office was used as a visitor centre. This had the advantage of keeping visitors off the site and also gave a good view of the work.

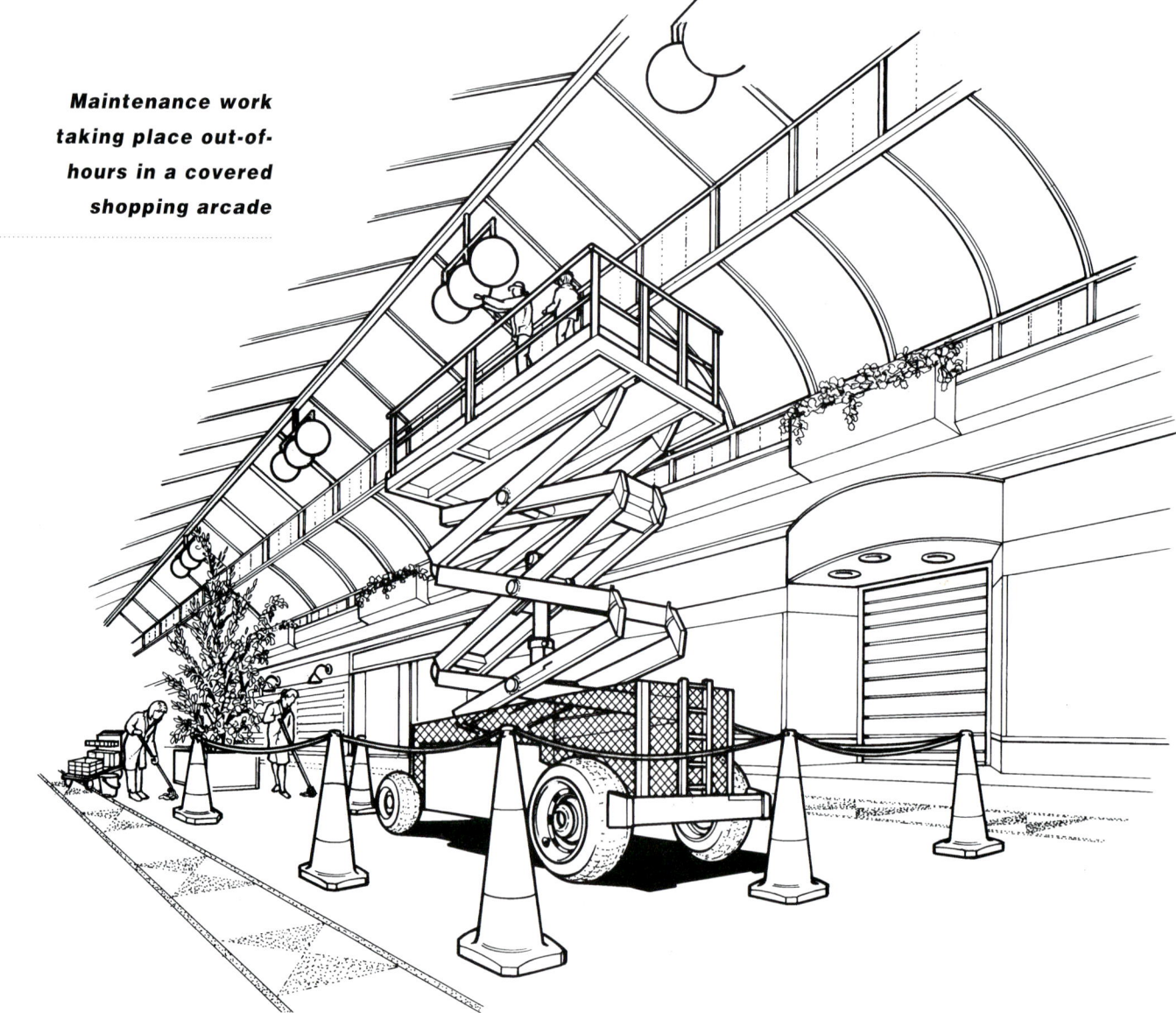

*Maintenance work taking place out-of-hours in a covered shopping arcade*

## OCCUPIED PREMISES

**75** Where construction work is carried out in, on or near occupied premises, for example houses, hospitals, factories, shops, etc, it may be necessary to evacuate part or all of the premises, either for the full duration of the work, or for a limited period. Regular clients such as housing associations and pub management companies often have an established policy which identifies the circumstances when it is appropriate to evacuate premises. The client should plan out the work in conjunction with the designers, contractors and, where CDM applies, the planning supervisor and principal contractor before deciding whether or not to evacuate. A number of factors need to be considered before a decision is made, including:

- the nature of the premises;
- who will be exposed;
- the extent and nature of the work;
- the associated risks to occupants;
- the time needed to complete the work;
- the significance of any risks associated with an evacuation;
- the costs of an evacuation, including alternative accommodation.

**76** These factors need to be weighed up at the planning stage and a decision made so that the contractor can identify the necessary precautions and develop the work programme accordingly. If the premises remain occupied, even partially, the risk to the occupants and the adequacy of the precautions should be reviewed as work progresses.

> **Consider the refurbishment of a pub. Vacating the premises has obvious advantages: it removes the public from the area of risk and allows the work to be completed quicker because contractors do not need to work around customers. There are equally obvious costs: loss of business and possible permanent loss of goodwill if regular customers find a permanent alternative. The decision whether or not to evacuate therefore depends chiefly on the extent and nature of the refurbishment and the significance of the risks to the public if they remain.**

**77** In certain premises however, the evacuation could itself be harmful, for example homes for the elderly. Here the client needs to decide whether their movement presents a greater risk than the construction work. In all cases, the right decision can only be made if the client and contractors liaise and pass on all the relevant information.

## REFURBISHMENT OF RESIDENTIAL PROPERTIES

**78** Sometimes it will be necessary to evacuate people during relatively short duration work, for example timber treatment or damp course work involving certain hazardous chemicals. Often these chemicals are injected into party (shared) walls and there have been instances where ill health with neighbours has been linked

# SECTION 5 — SELECTED GROUPS AND PREMISES WHICH NEED SPECIAL ATTENTION

with such work. The risk assessment should identify whether aspects of the work, for example the amount of the chemical to be injected or the nature of the party wall, makes it necessary to evacuate the neighbours as well. If the neighbours are to remain in residence they should be informed of the nature of the work.

**79** However, it is likely that residents will remain in occupation during most minor construction work such as re-glazing or painting. Indeed this might also include times when residents choose not to move out even when it would be preferable if they did. In these circumstances, the precautions will need to be re-considered to ensure the risks to the occupants (and the workers) are properly controlled. Separating the residents from the work, storage of materials and preventing unauthorised use of scaffolding and other access equipment - particularly by children - can present the main health and safety problems. Residents may also be concerned about the security of their property.

> A contractor left several short lengths of unsecured scaffold tube propped against a wall in a corridor in a block of flats. The stack moved and fell across the corridor as a resident was passing with a push chair and child. The resident was badly bruised by the falling tubes but the child escaped injury.

**80** Good communication between clients, contractors and residents is an important means of controlling the risks and minimising discomfort. It can also be essential when arranging alternative escape routes during work. Advice should be sought from the local fire authority where it is necessary to block or alter the permanent escape routes.

**81** The client should pass information to residents at a very early stage. Where a residents' association does not exist, the client should consider appointing a liaison officer to deal with the contractors. The principal contractor should also appoint someone to act as a focal point for dealings with the residents and their representatives. The identity of these people and how they can be contacted should be publicised.

**82** The principal contractor can take a number of steps to help reduce the risk. These include:

- sending information to each household outlining the nature of the work before it starts. An additional questionnaire can request any relevant information specific to that household such as special access requirements for disabled residents;

- providing all site workers with an identification card (preferably one with a photograph);

- ensuring that access to balconies, scaffolds, etc, is prevented or properly controlled;

- providing and marking alternative routes, for example by using orange plastic netting during working hours where necessary;

- providing fans and covered walkways if there is a risk that residents will be struck by falling materials.

**REFURBISHMENT OF INDUSTRIAL OR COMMERCIAL PROPERTIES**

83  Where work takes place within occupied factories, offices, shops and other premises, the client and the principal contractor will need to manage not only the risks created by their own work, they will also need to co-operate closely to manage those created by sharing the workplace. Where CDM applies, the client needs to pass relevant information, on to the planning supervisor and design team. This should be included in the pre-tender stage health and safety plan.

*Repairs to a city centre office showing fan and protected scaffold tubes*

84  Where CDM does not apply, joint agreements between the occupiers and contractors are still needed to ensure health and safety risks and precautions are properly managed and co-ordinated. It will be useful to nominate someone, perhaps the company health and safety officer to co-ordinate activities at relevant interfaces. Agreements should cover areas such as:

- respective responsibilities;
- mechanisms of co-operation and co-ordination;
- providing information about risks;
- controlling access to the areas where construction works are being carried out;
- emergency procedures.

> A chemical company had its car park re-surfaced. They provided the principal contractor with details of the substances manufactured and their risks as well as information about the fire alarm warning system and assembly points.

# SECTION 5: SELECTED GROUPS AND PREMISES WHICH NEED SPECIAL ATTENTION

**85** In some cases, the occupiers of premises may either prohibit or restrict the types of activity which can be carried out on certain parts of the construction site.

> A new waste processing unit was being installed in a sewage treatment works (STW). The client knew that the waste treatment process could cause flammable concentrations of methane gas to be produced in some areas of the STW. The client therefore prohibited the use of welding equipment and other sources of ignition on certain parts of the construction site and imposed a PTW system on contractors for hot works on other parts of the site.

**86** Sometimes work is carried out in areas which need to remain occupied. The risk assessment should indicate the nature of the perimeters and how they will be maintained. It might be possible for the work to take place outside normal hours. Alternatively, a physical barrier may be necessary to separate the construction work. The highest standards should be adopted where work is carried out above a public area. This will mean taking steps to prevent materials falling in the first place and then excluding people from the area below the work or providing adequate fans, tunnels, etc. Post suitable warning signs around the area.

> A company which was painting and decorating an office did some work in a stairwell at the weekend to maintain a fire escape during the week and minimise inconvenience.

## HEALTH CARE PREMISES

**87** In health care premises, the vulnerability of those who are within the premises or likely to visit that area is an important additional concern. Visitors might include children, and out-patients with restricted mobility or with partial sight, etc. Also, bear in mind that patients and visitors may be in a distressed condition or distracted by health concerns.

> Some patients, such as those who have had major surgery, will be more open to infection than healthy people. Be aware that refurbishment works may disturb fungal spores and other organisms which could be a serious hazard to patients but which would not affect others.
>
> In a psychiatric hospital, the client decided there was a risk that some of the patients might try to climb on to a traditional scaffold out of hours. The principal contractor therefore used mobile elevating work platforms instead. These were isolated at the end of the working day to prevent unauthorised use.

**88** Avoid creating unnecessary obstructions such as trailing leads on stairways, ladders in corridors and poorly parked delivery vehicles. As well as the obvious hazards, they may well impede those who need to gain access through hospital buildings or grounds in an emergency. Control any necessary obstructions by warning everyone likely to be affected well in advance. Provide alternative access routes, clear warning signs and barriers where appropriate. Always clear obstructions as quickly as possible. Check that plant, equipment and materials are stored safely at the end of the shift.

**89** Separate site vehicles and pedestrians from the hospital traffic as much as possible. Make sure routes to the site are clearly signposted. If hospital traffic and visitors have to be re-routed during work, make sure the new access routes are also clearly marked.

## HOUSE BUILDING

**90** House building presents a particular problem because often parts of the new estate will become occupied as others are still being constructed. Liaison with new occupiers will be important, and the sales staff and contractors need to work closely together. The location of the show home and associated sales office can help keep purchasers and prospective purchasers of property on the housing development away from the construction work.

**91** The perimeter between the site and the occupied area will usually change as the work progresses. Arrangements for maintaining the perimeter and other precautions need to reflect the speed of change within the site and the risks. Whether the construction site needs to be physically separated from the new residents depends on the likelihood that the public will want to come on to the site or stray there by accident and the consequences if they do. For example, if the new residents include young children who may play on the site, then a 2 metre fence should be provided and maintained. However, where the work is carried out in an area of the construction site which is remote from the new occupied houses and the population does not include children, then simpler fencing or other measures such as tape and warning signs might prove adequate.

**92** Separating plant and vehicles from the public can also become difficult. If possible, construct new roads as early as possible or create alternative routes to avoid using plant and equipment on the same roads as new occupiers. If this cannot be done, keep their use by site traffic to an absolute minimum; institute and maintain low speeds. Provide clearly signed one way systems where possible.

> A project involved the construction of a new road and the phased construction of new houses. The client specified that the new road had to be complete before work on the housing entered the second phase. At the start of the second phase, the work area was redefined, the perimeter fence was moved and site vehicles were prohibited from using the new road.

**93** Housekeeping is particularly important on sites which are partially occupied and partially under construction. At the end of the day, make sure that ladders are removed, materials stacked properly, and that plant is isolated, etc. Make maximum use of the compound for storing equipment and materials outside normal working hours.

# SECTION 5
## SELECTED GROUPS AND PREMISES WHICH NEED SPECIAL ATTENTION

APPENDIX

# Identifying the hazards and evaluating risks

# APPENDIX: IDENTIFYING THE HAZARDS AND EVALUATING RISKS

**INTRODUCTION**

1  Protecting the public from the risks created by construction work should be a fundamental objective of any construction project. The effect which the construction work may have on the public should be considered during the design, planning and implementation stages of the project. The earlier the risks to the public are considered, the easier it usually is to eliminate hazards and control risks. But remember, it is necessary to review and, if required, revise the control measures as the work progresses.

2  The process of systematically identifying significant hazards, determining who could be affected and evaluating what risk the hazards pose in practice is called risk assessment. Elimination of hazards and control of risk is the key to good health and safety management. This section explains how the principles of risk management may be applied to protect the public and visitors from construction activities. The principles are illustrated using two examples set out as a flow chart.

**RISK ASSESSMENT**

This section illustrates the risk assessment process using two worked examples.

3  The risk assessment process can be broken down into five steps.

**Step 1: Identify the hazards**

A hazard is any event which has the potential to cause harm, for example exposure to a harmful substance. Unless hazards are identified it is unlikely that risks will be properly controlled. This is a vital first step.

| EXAMPLE A | EXAMPLE B |
|---|---|
| **Statue cleaning** | **City centre office renewal** |
| Statues in a busy covered shopping precinct need to be acid cleaned periodically. | The roof of an old Victorian office in a city centre requires total renewal. This will be done using a full traditional scaffold. This example only considers the hazard of erecting the scaffold. It does not include work on the roof. |

**Step 2: Who may be harmed, how and when?**

Decide whether members of the public may be affected by these hazards. Consider how and when they might be harmed, and for how long.

| EXAMPLE A | EXAMPLE B |
|---|---|
| **Statue cleaning** | **City centre office renewal** |
| Anyone who gets the chemical solution on their skin is exposed to the hazard. If a child climbed on to the statue and later rubbed their eyes with their fingers this would clearly aggravate any problems. It can also create a nuisance if it splashes on to clothing. | People can be struck by scaffolding components during the erection, handling and movement of the scaffolding when it is delivered to the site. |

**Step 3:
Evaluate the risks
and consider how
the risk of injury or
ill health can be
reduced**

Having identified the hazards and who might be affected, you then need to evaluate how likely it is that harm will occur (i.e. the **risk**).

### EXAMPLE A
#### Statue cleaning
The hazard is exposure to the chemical on the statue. Children climbing on to the statue in a shopping precinct can be considered especially at risk. In considering the risk, you will need to think about the strength of the solution and its harmful effects. How harmful this is, the number of people who could be exposed and the length of their exposure.

### EXAMPLE B
#### City centre office renewal
Members of the public are exposed to scaffolding components when the scaffold is being delivered, handled and erected. The risk will be at the greatest when there are large numbers of the public around and if they are allowed to pass underneath or immediately adjacent to the scaffold when it is being erected.

This information allows you to decide what measures need to be taken to eliminate the hazards or control the risks to members of the public and visitors. The precautions which you need to take will depend on the significance of the risk, for example the nature of the chemical to which people are exposed, the likelihood that people will be exposed, how many people could be affected, and the consequences if they are exposed. There are certain principles to follow when making your decision:

* Always consider if the hazard can be eliminated altogether by using a different working method, or materials.

### EXAMPLE A
#### Statue cleaning
Can the statues be left untreated; or alternatively treated by a substance which eliminates the acid treatment? Can a less hazardous substance be used?

### EXAMPLE B
#### City centre office renewal
Schedule the work when there are fewer people around. Provide alternative routes away from the scaffolding which are clearly signposted or if a covered walkway or thoroughfare for the scaffold is to be incorporated then ensure that it is constructed first.

* If the hazard cannot be eliminated, control it at source.

### EXAMPLE A
#### Statue cleaning
Can the work be done out of hours? Ensure that a suitable fence is provided around the work, and have regard to any tripping hazard the feet of the fence may create.

### EXAMPLE B
#### City centre office renewal
Fully board and protect lifts as you progress. Consider boxing the components and using mechanical lifting equipment to various lifts. Ensure that those carrying out the work are trained and familiar with working in such an environment.

# APPENDIX    IDENTIFYING THE HAZARDS AND EVALUATING RISKS

\* If the hazard cannot be controlled at source, develop an approach which will provide maximum protection for the maximum number of people, irrespective of any special equipment, training or work process.

**EXAMPLE A**
### Statue cleaning
Can the statue be removed to be cleaned off site?

**EXAMPLE B**
### City centre office renewal
Create an exclusion zone to keep the public out of the area where components may be dropped during handling.

**Step 4: Record your significant findings, and where necessary what you intend to do and why**

Recording the information obtained during the assessment process is often an important part of managing the risks. The detail should however be proportionate to the risks: lengthy or complex records are rarely helpful. Risk assessments do not always need to be written. If, for example, you have less than five people working under your control, it should be possible to just discuss the findings. But even in these circumstances writing it down can still help. So where CDM applies, this approach will be valuable in developing parts of the construction phase health and safety plan.

**EXAMPLE A**
### Statue cleaning
A record of the control measures for the use of the chemical may help. Information should be available in the event of spillage or emergency. Those carrying out the work should be trained. Control over the size/amount of chemicals used can have other advantages, for example manual handling, environmental and wastage risks can be reduced.

**EXAMPLE B**
### City centre office renewal
A generic approach by the contractor may well be appropriate, however, bespoking the assessment could be required in new/unusual circumstances.

**Step 5: Review and revise your assessment where appropriate**

Check your assessment and the validity of the assumption you made as the work progresses to make sure your precautions remain appropriate. Valuable lessons can also be learned by carrying out a review of general health and safety performance at the end of each job. This allows you to identify and build upon approaches which have worked as well as learning from those which have not. But again keep it simple and proportionate to the risks involved.

**EXAMPLE A**
### Statue cleaning
New substances/treatments may come on to the market, or further information may emerge about the current chemical you are using; this may well require you to change.

**EXAMPLE B**
### City centre office renewal
If you have a number of incidents (for example, where components are dropped during erection or dismantling), you will need to review your assessment. Consider changes in procedures, times and approaches to the work, such as organising road closures.

**WHO DOES WHAT?**

4    Everyone involved in construction work can help control risks. Clients, planners and designers may often have vital information about hazards. They may also control or influence how and when contractors carry out the work. Relevant health and safety information should be given to all parties who need it. This is essential if hazards are to be identified and risks properly controlled.

## FURTHER READING

*A guide to managing health and safety in construction*  HSE Books 1995
ISBN 0 7176 0755 0

*A guide to risk assessment requirements*  IND(G)218L HSE Books 1996

*A short guide to the Personal Protective Equipment at Work Regulations 1992*
IND(G)174L  HSE Books 1995

*A step-by-step guide to COSHH assessment*  HS(G)97 HSE Books 1993
ISBN 0 11 886379 7

*British Standards Institution Code of Practice for safe use of cranes*  BS 7121
Part 1: *General*  1996
Part 2: *Inspection, testing and examinations* 1991

*Contractors in schools: information to headteachers, school governors and bursars*  IACL98 HSE Books 1996 (available from HSE offices)

*Construction (head protection) Regulations 1989*  HSE Books 1990

*Dust and noise in the construction process*  CRR73  HSE Books 1995
ISBN 0 7176 0768 2

*Electrical safety on construction sites*  HS(G)141 HSE Books 1995
ISBN 0 7176 1000 4

*Everyone's guide to RIDDOR '95*  HSE 31  HSE Books 1996 (single copies are free; the leaflet is also available in priced packs of 10 from HSE Books ISBN 0 7176 1077 2)

*First aid at work - your questions answered*  IND(G)214L HSE Books 1997

*5 steps to risk assessment*  IND(G)163L HSE Books 1994

*General COSHH ACOP and Carcinogens ACOP and Biological Agents ACOP (1996 edition) Control of Substances Hazardous to Health Regulations 1994*
L5 HSE Books 1997  ISBN 0 7176 1308 9

*Health and Safety at Work etc Act 1974: Advice to employers*  HSC3
HSE Books 1975

*Health and Safety at Work etc Act 1974: The Act outlined*  HSC2  HSE Books 1975

*Health and safety in construction*  HS(G)150  HSE Books 1996  ISBN 0 7176 1143 4

*Information on site safety for designers of smaller building projects*  CRR 72
HSE 1995  ISBN 0 7176 0777 1

*Lighting at work*  HS(G)38  HSE Books 1987  ISBN 0 7176 0467 5

*Managing asbestos in workplace buildings*  IND(G)223L HSE Books 1996
ISBN 0 7176 1179 5

*Managing construction for health and safety. Construction (Design and Management) Regulations 1994 Approved Code of Practice* L54 HSE Books 1995 ISBN 0 7176 0792 5

*Noise in construction* IND(G)127L HSE Books 1992

*Personal protective equipment* Construction Information Sheets
    No. 28 PPE: *Principles, duties and responsibilities* HSE Books 1993
    No. 29 PPE: *Head protection* HSE Books 1993
    No. 30 PPE: *Hearing protection* HSE Books 1993
    No. 31 PPE: *Eye and face protection* HSE Books 1993
    No. 32 PPE: *Respiratory protective equipment* HSE Books 1993
    No. 33 PPE: *General and specialist clothing* HSE Books 1993
    No. 34 PPE: *Gloves* HSE Books 1993
    No. 35 PPE: *Safety footwear* HSE Books 1993

*Protection of workers and the general public during the development of contaminated land* HS(G)66 HSE Books 1991 ISBN 0 11 885657 X

*Reversing vehicles* IND(G)148L HSE Books 1993 ISBN 0 7176 1063 2

*Safe erection of structures* Guidance note GS 28
Part 2: *Site management and procedures* HSE Books 1985 ISBN 0 11 883605 6

*Safety at street works and road works* A Code of Practice issued by the Secretaries of State for Transport, Scotland and Wales under sections 65 and 124 of the New Roads and Street Works Act 1991 HMSO 1992 ISBN 0 11 551144 X

*Temporarily suspended access cradles and platforms* Construction Information Sheet No. 5 HSE Books 1995

*Work equipment Provision and Use of Work Equipment Regulations 1992: Guidance on Regulations* L22 HSE Books 1992 ISBN 0 7176 0414 4

*Workplace transport safety - guidance for employers* HS(G)136 HSE Books 1995 ISBN 0 7176 0935 9

*Young people at work* HS(G)165 HSE Books 1997 ISBN 0 7176 1285 6

**ADDITIONAL INFORMATION**

A video called *Game over* (1997) is available from CFL Vision, PO Box 35, Wetherby LS23 7EX

Printed and published by the Health and Safety Executive
**C100** **6/97**